QUILTS

CHEERFUL

by Christiane Meunier, Shelley Knapp, Mary Russell and more!

Moon over
MOUNTAIN
2 Public Avenue,
Montrose, PA 18801-1220
www.QuiltTownUSA.com

CONTENTS

Moon Over Mountain
2 Public Avenue
Montrose, Pennsylvania 18801-1220

First Printing: 2005

Library of Congress Cataloging-in-Publication Data
Meunier, Christiane.
  Cheerful quilts/ by Christiane Meunier, Shelley Knapp, Mary Russell, and others.
    p.cm.
  ISBN 1-885588-71-2 (pbk.)
  1. Quilts—Patterns. 2. Patchwork—Patterns. I. Knapp, Shelley, date- II. Russell, Mary, date- III. Title.
  TT835.M4853 2005
  746.46'041—dc22
                    2005023639

Design and Illustrations..Diane Albeck-Grick
Photography....................Van Zandbergen Photography,
                        Brackney, Pennsylvania

Our Mission Statement
We publish quality quilting books that recognize, promote, and inspire self-expression. We are dedicated to serving our customers with respect, kindness, and efficiency.

www.QuiltTownUSA.com

ABOUT THE QUILTMAKERS

Christiane Meunier, author of 12 popular quilting books, has been a leader in the quilt world since publishing *Quilting Today* magazine in 1987. She has also earned acclaim as a quilt designer whose works have been featured in numerous publications and shows. Christiane's incredible sense of color guides her to create quilts that speak to all who view them. To learn more about Christiane, visit www.QuiltTownUSA.com.

Mary Russell, a self-acclaimed "Local Quilt Goddess" living on the Central Coast of California, has been quilting since 1976. In May 1994, she developed a ruler that makes rotary cutting pieces for Double Wedding Ring quilts fast and easy. Today Mary continues to teach workshops and sells her rulers all across the country. To learn more about Mary and her rulers, visit www.mary-russell.com.

Shelley Knapp has been quilting since the early 1980's. A self-taught artist, her passion for color led her to join her husband, Randy, in making kaleidoscopes, and in creating bright and beautiful quilts. She is also an accomplished long-arm machine quilter and strives to make every quilt as beautiful as possible. To learn more about Shelley, visit www.knappstudios.com.

Mary Harmon of Syracuse, New York has been quilting since 1987, when she and her sister took a quilting class at a local high school. Her quilts tend to be more traditional, but she loves to learn new techniques and styles. She professes that "my specialty seems to be UFO's, since there is always something new to try before I can finish my last quilt".

Claudia Clark Myers has been sewing for many years. First in her background with costume design and construction, and for the past 12 years in quilting. Her vision of color and the use of many fabrics, makes her quilts beautiful and unique. For more information about Claudia, visit www.2muchfunquilting.com/.

Cheryl Kagen has been quilting since 1973. She specializes in miniature quilts, but occasionally makes full-size scrap quilts. She has recently started to make fabric masterpieces in her Seneca, New York home in the form of art quilts.

KING BALI

Quilt Size: 96" x 102"   **Block Size: 6" square**

MATERIALS

- Light batiks totaling at least 9 yards
- Dark batiks totaling at least 4 yards
- 1 yard dark batik for the binding
- 9 yards backing fabric
- 100" x 106" piece of batting

CUTTING

Dimensions include a 1/4" seam allowance.

- Cut 272: 4 7/8" squares, assorted light batiks, then cut each square in half diagonally
- Cut 816: 2 1/2" squares in 272 matching sets of 3, assorted light batiks
- Cut 272: 4 1/8" squares, assorted dark batiks, then cut each square in quarters diagonally

Also:

- Cut 11: 2 1/2" x 40" strips, dark batik, for the binding

DIRECTIONS

1. Lay out 3 matching 2 1/2" light squares and 4 matching dark triangles. Sew them into 3 sections and join the sections.

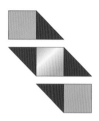

2. Sew 2 light triangles to the pieced unit to complete a block. Make 272.

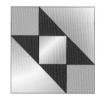

3. Referring to the photo, lay out the blocks in 17 rows of 16.
4. Sew the blocks into rows and join the rows.
5. Finish the quilt as described in the *General Directions*, using the 2 1/2" x 40" dark batik strips for the binding.

ALTERNATE SIZE CHART FOR KING BALI			
Quilt Size	72" x 84"	66" square	36" x 42"
Number of blocks	168	121	42
Assorted lights	5 1/2 yards	4 1/4 yards	1 3/4 yards
Assorted darks	2 1/2 yards	1 3/4 yards	3/4 yard
Binding	3/4 yard	5/8 yard	1/2 yard

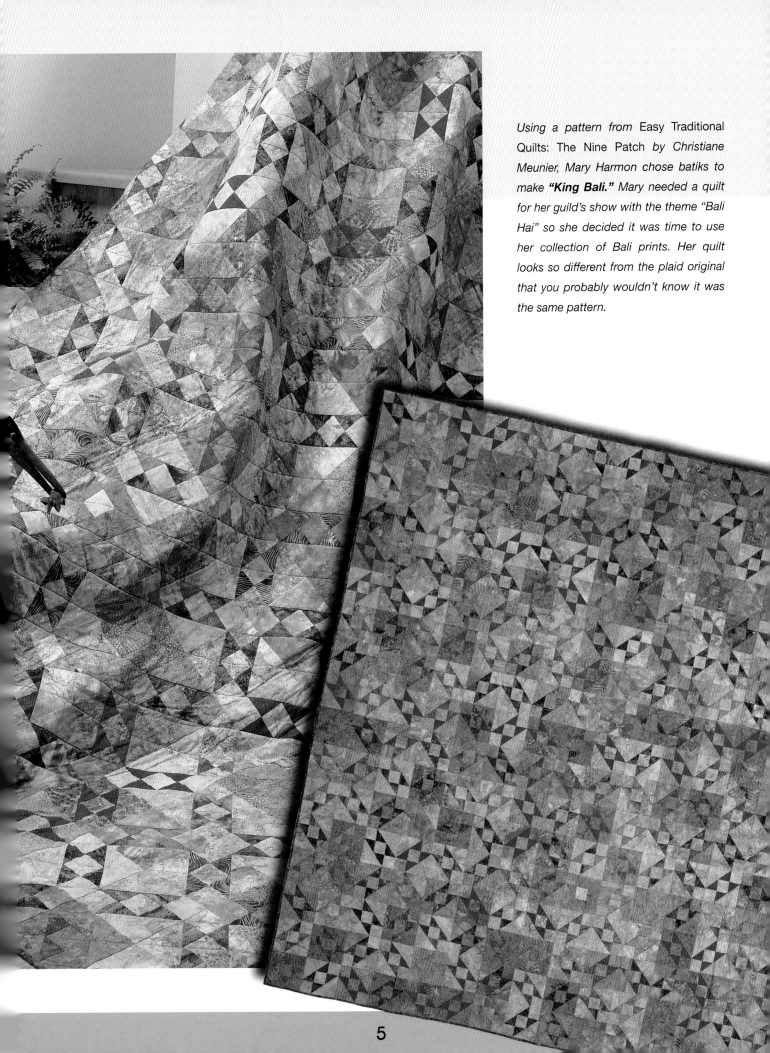

Using a pattern from Easy Traditional Quilts: The Nine Patch *by Christiane Meunier, Mary Harmon chose batiks to make* **"King Bali."** *Mary needed a quilt for her guild's show with the theme "Bali Hai" so she decided it was time to use her collection of Bali prints. Her quilt looks so different from the plaid original that you probably wouldn't know it was the same pattern.*

OUT OF THE BOX

Quilt Size: 87 1/2" x 58 3/4"   **Block Size: 7 1/4" triangle**

MATERIALS

- Assorted light prints, totaling at least 2 1/4 yards
- Assorted medium prints totaling at least 2 1/4 yards
- Assorted dark prints totaling at least 2 1/4 yards
- Assorted red batiks for the outer edge totaling at least 2 1/2 yards
- 3/4 yard dark red for the binding
- 5 1/4 yards backing fabric
- 63" x 92" piece of batting

CUTTING

Dimensions include a 1/4" seam allowance.

- Cut 25: 4 1/2" x 20" strips, assorted prints (8 dark, 9 medium, and 8 light), then cut six 60° triangles from each strip (small triangles) NOTE: *Keep them separated in 3 stacks by value.*

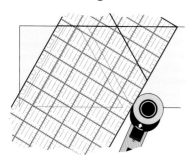

- Cut 4: 5 3/4" x 18" strips, (2 darks, one medium, and one light) then cut four 60° triangles from each strip (large triangles for the 4 maverick cubes)
- Cut 50: 1 3/4" x 20" strips, assorted light prints in 25 matching pairs
- Cut 50: 1 3/4" x 20" strips, assorted medium prints, in 25 matching pairs
- Cut 54: 1 3/4" x 20" strips, assorted dark prints, in 27 matching pairs
- Cut 6: 4 1/2" x 20" strips, assorted red batiks, then cut six 60° triangles from each strip
- Cut 36: 1 3/4" x 20" strips, assorted red batiks
- Cut 4: 6 3/4" x 15 3/8" rectangles, red batik
- Cut 4: 7" x 40" strips, red batik
- Cut 8: 2 1/2" x 40" strips, dark red, for the binding

DIRECTIONS

The directions are written as if each block uses matching pieces, but you might want to mix them up a bit for variety. Just be careful of correct value placement.

1. From the small triangles, choose 2 matching dark triangles, 2 matching medium triangles and 2 matching light triangles.

Lay them out as shown.

2. Choose two 1 3/4" x 20" matching light strips, 2 matching medium strips, and 2 matching dark strips. Cut each strip into two 10" sections.

3. You will sew strips to the small triangles in the following manner: Sew a 10" strip to one side, allowing approximately 1 1/2" extra at the bottom edge and the remainder of the strip extending past the top, as shown. Trim the ends of the strip even with the edges of the triangle.

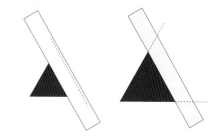

Sew the matching 10" strip to the triangle and trim.

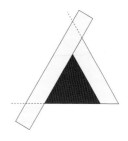

4. Sew strips to the six triangles. Be sure to sew the light strips to the triangles on the top, the medium strips to the triangles on the left, and the dark strips to the triangles on the right.

5. Sew the units into 2 half-blocks, as shown. Do not join the sections yet. Stack them and set them aside. Make 23.

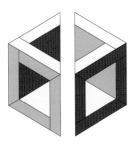

6. Make 12 half-blocks in the same manner, using only small red triangles and red strips.

7. Sew dark strips to a small medium-value triangle as described in Step 3 on page 6. Make 4 matching pairs.

8. From the large triangles, lay out 2 dark triangles, one medium triangle, and one light triangle. Place a pair of triangles from Step 7 into the layout.

9. Cut the remaining 1 3/4" x 20" strips into 10" sections. You will sew a strip to one side of the large triangles only. Sew matching light strips to the triangles on the top, and matching medium strips to the triangles on the left.

10. Sew the triangle units into 2 half-blocks, as before. Make 4 sets.

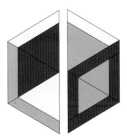

(continued on page 11)

TANGE-URPLE

Quilt Size: 95 1/2" square   **Block Size: 12 3/4" square**

MATERIALS

- Assorted purple, pink, orange, and red prints totaling at least 2 yards
- 16 assorted orange prints each at least 8" x 11"
- 25 assorted purple prints each at least 7 1/2" x 15"
- 2 1/4 yards beige print
- 1/2 yard orange print for the middle border
- 5 1/2 yards purple for the sashing, borders, and binding
- 8 1/2 yards backing fabric
- 100" square of batting

CUTTING

Dimensions include a 1/4" seam allowance.

From the assorted purple, pink, orange, and red prints:
- Cut 164: 2" squares, in 82 matching pairs
- Cut 100: 2" squares, in 25 sets of 4
- Cut 50: 4 1/2" squares, in 25 matching pairs

From each of the 16 orange prints:
- Cut 12: 2 5/8" squares

From each of the 25 purple prints:
- Cut 2: 7 1/4" squares, then cut them in half diagonally to

yield 100 triangles

From the beige:
- Cut 66: 4 1/2" squares, then cut 16 of them in quarters diagonally to yield 64 triangles
- Cut 100: 2" squares
- Cut 100: 2" x 3 1/2" rectangles

From the orange print border fabric:
- Cut 9: 1 1/2" x 40" strips

From the purple:
- Cut 4: 5" x 98" lengthwise strips
- Cut 4: 2 1/2" x 86" lengthwise strips
- Cut 80: 2 5/8" x 13 1/4" strips
- Cut 10: 2 1/2" x 40" strips, for the binding

DIRECTIONS

1. Choose 2 pairs of 2" squares. Sew them together to make a Four Patch, as shown. Make 41. Set them aside.

2. Sew a 2" beige square to a 2" print square. Sew a 2" x 3 1/2" beige rectangle to the unit to make a corner unit. Make 25 matching sets of 4. Set them aside.

3. Draw a diagonal line from corner to corner on the wrong side of each 4 1/2" beige square.

(continued on page 10)

Accepting a challenge from her husband, Shelley Knapp used only fabric from her stash (with the exception of the border fabric, which came from a friend's stash) to make *"Tange-urple."* Even the backing was pieced from leftover fabrics. Shelley was inspired by a Debbie Caffrey mystery quilt for the blocks and Sharyn Craig for the secondary-design setting. As a professional long-arm machine quilter, Shelley says the quilting was easy. The design came to her as she was piecing the quilt top.

(continued from page 8)

4. Place a marked square on a 4 1/2" print square, right sides together. Sew 1/4" away from the drawn line on both sides. Make 2 using matching prints.

5. Cut on the drawn lines to yield 4 pieced squares. Press the seam allowances toward the print.

6. On the wrong side of 2 pieced squares, continue the drawn line on the print side.

7. Place a marked pieced square on an unmarked pieced square, right sides together with beige against print. Sew 1/4" away from the line on both sides. Make 2.

8. Cut on the drawn lines to yield 4 Hour Glass units. Make 25 sets of 4. Trim each unit to 3 1/2" square.

9. Choose 4 Hour Glass units, 4 corner units, and a Four Patch. Lay them out, as shown. Sew the units into rows and join the rows to make a block center. Make 25.

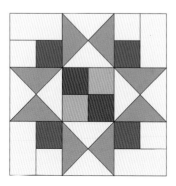

10. Sew 2 purple print triangles to opposite sides of a block center. Press the seam allowances toward the triangles. Sew 2 matching triangles to the remaining sides to complete a block. Make 25.

11. Sew 4 beige triangles to each of the remaining Four Patches to make 16 cornerstones.

ASSEMBLY

1. Lay out the blocks in 5 rows of 5. Place pairs of 2 5/8" x 13 1/4" purple strips and the cornerstones between the blocks. Refer to the photo and the following diagram. Do not join the blocks and strips yet.

2. Draw a diagonal line from corner to corner on the wrong side of 12 matching 2 5/8" orange squares.

3. Place a marked square on the bottom right corner of the first block. Sew on the marked line. Press the square toward the corner, aligning the edges. Trim the seam allowance to 1/4". Place the block back in the layout.

4. Remove the first set of vertical strips. Sew a marked orange square to the bottom of each strip, as shown. Press and trim, as before. Sew the strips together to make a sashing unit and place it back in the layout.

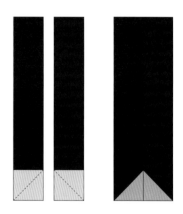

5. Working around the first cornerstone, sew orange squares to the adjacent blocks and sashing strips in the same manner, placing them back into the layout after completing each unit.

6. Sew orange squares to each of the remaining blocks and sashing strips, referring to the photo as necessary.

7. Sew the blocks and sashing units into rows. Join the rows.

8. Measure the width of the quilt. Trim two 2 1/2" x 86" purple strips to that measurement. Sew them to opposite sides of the quilt.

9. Measure the length of the quilt, including the borders. Trim the remaining 2 1/2" x 86" purple strips to that measurement and sew them to the quilt.

10. Sew the 1 1/2" x 40" orange strips together, end to end. Measure the quilt and cut 2 lengths from the orange strip each equal to that measurement. Sew them to opposite sides of the quilt.

11. Measure the quilt and cut 2 orange lengths to that measurement. Sew them to the remaining sides of the quilt.

12. Measure the quilt and trim the 5" x 98" purple strips to fit. Sew them to the quilt.

13. Finish the quilt as described in the *General Directions*, using the 2 1/2" x 40" purple strips for the binding.

OUT OF THE BOX (continued from page 7)

ASSEMBLY

1. Referring to the Assembly Diagram, lay out the half-blocks for each block. Pay careful attention to the direction of the blocks.

2. Place two 7" x 40" red batik strips right sides together. Straighten one end. Move the ruler over 1" and make a 60° cut. Move the ruler over 1" again and cut as shown. You will have 4 edge pieces. Repeat to cut a total of 28.

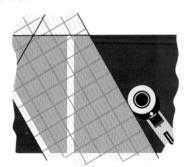

3. Trim the ends of the 6 3/4" x 15 3/8" red rectangles at a 60° angle from the bottom corners to make a trapezoid, as shown.

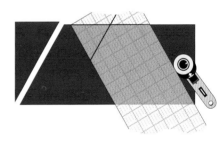

4. Place the red trapezoids and red half-blocks at the left and right sides of the layout. Place the red edge pieces at the top and bottom of the vertical rows.

5. Sew the pieces into vertical rows and join the rows.

6. Finish the quilt as described in the *General Directions*, using the 2 1/2" x 40" dark red strips for the binding.

Assembly Diagram

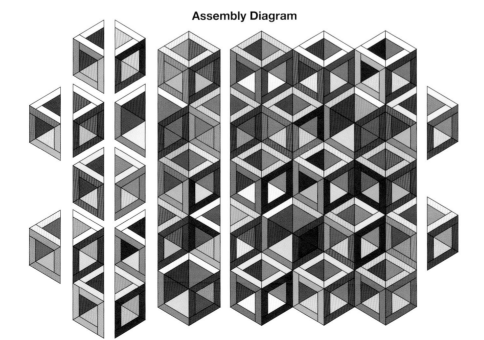

FOOLING AROUND

Quilt Size: 62 1/2" square   **Block Size: 7 1/2" square**

MATERIALS

- Scraps of light, medium, and dark hand-dyed fabrics totaling at least 6 yards
- 3/4 yard medium blue for the binding
- 4 yards backing fabric
- 67" square of batting
- 4 strips of freezer paper, each measuring 5 1/2" x 65", for the border foundations

CUTTING

Dimensions include a 1/4" seam allowance.

- Cut squares, rectangles, and strips of assorted light, medium, and dark hand-dyed fabrics as you piece the blocks.
- Cut 7: 2 1/2" x 40" strips, medium blue, for the binding

DIRECTIONS

For the blocks:

1. Piece together squares, rectangles, and strips of assorted hand-dyed fabrics into a unit large enough so you can cut an 8" square from it. Make forty-nine 8" blocks. Refer to the quilt photo as necessary.

For the borders:

1. Fold a 5 1/2" x 65" strip of paper in half to mark the center. Measure 26 1/4" from the center mark on both sides and mark the paper.

2. Draw a triangle at each end inside the marks, as shown.

3. Fill in the center by drawing additional triangles, varying the sizes and shapes. Make 4 foundations.

4. Foundation piece each border according to the *General Directions*. You'll begin and end each foundation with a large piece of fabric. These pieces will be mitered after the borders are sewn to the quilt.

5. Trim the fabric 1/4" beyond the edges of the paper foundaation.

ASSEMBLY

1. Lay out the blocks in 7 rows of 7. Sew the blocks into rows and join the rows.

2. Center and sew the borders to the sides of the quilt. Start, stop and backstitch 1/4" from the edges of the quilt.

3. Remove the paper from the borders and miter the corners.

4. Finish the quilt as described in the *General Directions*, using the 2 1/2" x 40" medium blue strips for the binding.

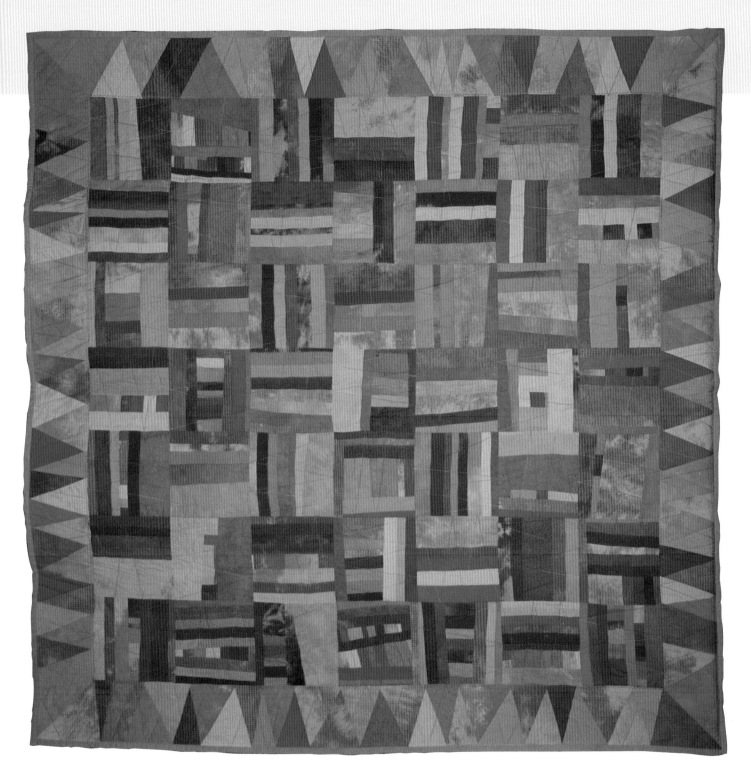

"Fooling Around" is a colorful creation of Mary Russell. Mary could not bear to throw away any of her hand-dyed fabric scraps, so even some of the strips within her quilt blocks are pieced. Mary says this quilt is a *"free-form delight"* right to the borders.

KALEIDOSCOPE

Quilt Size: 83 1/2" x 96 1/2"   **Block Size: 13" square**

MATERIALS

- Assorted dark batiks totaling at least 4 yards
- Assorted light batiks totaling at least 3 yards
- 3 1/4 yards purple batik for the inner and outer borders, and binding
- 3/4 yard light batik for the middle border
- 7 1/2 yards backing fabric
- 88" x 101" piece of batting

CUTTING

Patterns (on page 17) are full size and include a 1/4" seam allowance as do all dimensions given.

- Cut 60: A triangles, light batiks
- Cut 60: B triangles, light batiks
- Cut 60: A triangles, dark batiks
- Cut 60: B triangles, dark batiks
- Cut 60: 4 1/8" squares, dark batiks, then cut them in half diagonally to yield 120 corner triangles
- Cut 4: 6 1/2" x 86" strips, purple batik, for the outer border
- Cut 2: 2 1/4" x 80" strips, purple batik, for the inner border
- Cut 2: 2 1/4" x 70" strips purple batik, for the inner border
- Cut 10: 2 1/2" x 40" purple

batik strips, for the binding
- Cut 8: 2" x 40" light batik strips, for the middle border

DIRECTIONS

For each of 15 dark blocks:
1. Choose 4 dark A triangles. Notice that in some blocks the triangles match and in other blocks they don't. Lay them out with 4 matching light B triangles. NOTE: *The light triangles don't have to match but they should be of the same color family.*

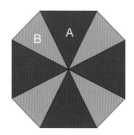

2. Sew the triangles into pairs and join the pairs.
3. Sew a dark corner triangle to each light B triangle to complete a block. Make 15.

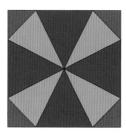

(continued on page 16)

Batiks from Bali Fabrics provide just the right contrast in **"Kaleido-scope."** Christiane Meunier says that the yellows are actually medium in value but they serve as lights in this design. The machine quilting was done by Shelley Knapp.

(continued from page 14)

4. Place the blocks on a design wall in 6 rows, as shown.

5. Starting in the upper left corner, place 4 light A triangles and 4 dark B triangles in the layout. Match the color family of the light triangles with the adjacent blocks.

6. Sew the triangles together, as before, then sew dark corner triangles to the dark B's to complete the block. Place the block into the layout.

7. Continue making alternate blocks, matching the light print triangles to the adjacent blocks.

ASSEMBLY

1. Sew the blocks into rows and join the rows.

2. Measure the length of the quilt. Trim the 2 1/4" x 80" purple batik strips to that measurement. Sew them to the sides of the quilt.

3. Measure the width of the quilt. Trim the 2 1/4" x 70" purple batik strips to that measurement. Sew them to the top and bottom of the quilt.

4. Sew the 2" x 40" light batik strips together, end to end, to make a long strip.

5. Measure the length of the quilt. Cut 2 lengths from the strip, each equal to that measurement, and sew them to the sides of the quilt.

6. Cut 2 lengths to fit the quilt's width and sew them to the top and bottom of the quilt.

7. Trim two 6 1/2" x 86" purple batik strips to fit the quilt's length and sew them to the sides of the quilt.

8. Trim the remaining 6 1/2" x 86" purple batik strips to fit the quilt's width and sew them to the top and bottom of the quilt.

9. Finish the quilt as described in the *General Directions*, using the 2 1/2" x 40" purple batik strips for the binding.

Coloring Diagram

Full-size patterns for Kaleidoscope *(The pattern begins on page 14.)*

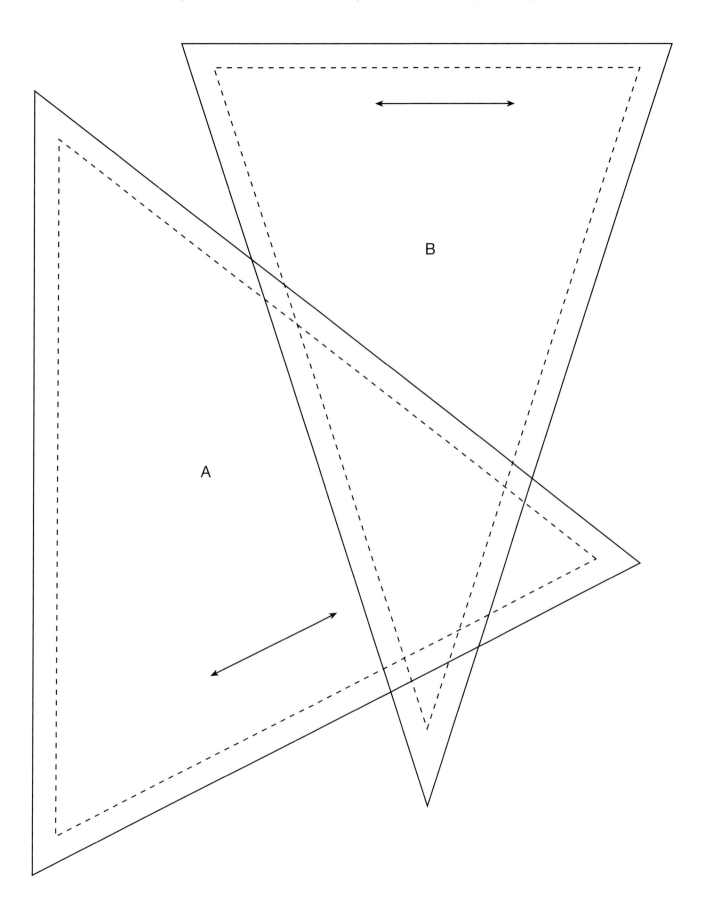

MOONSHINE

Quilt Size: 92" x 99 1/2"   **Block Size: 7 1/2" square**

MATERIALS

- Assorted light, medium, and dark prints totaling at least 16 yards, in 1/4 yard to 1/2 yard pieces
- 3/4 yard stripe for the inner border
- 1 7/8 yards dark print for the outer border and binding
- 8 1/4 yards backing fabric
- 96" x 104" piece of batting
- Paper for the foundations
- Clear template plastic

CUTTING

Dimensions include a 1/4" seam allowance.

- Cut 11: 2 1/2" x 40" cross-wise strips, stripe, for the inner border
- Cut 11: 3 1/4" x 40" strips, dark print, for the outer border
- Cut 11: 2 1/2" x 40" strips, dark print, for the binding
- Cut 16: 8" squares, assorted prints, for the plain squares

DIRECTIONS

For each foundation choose one shade of leaf and one shade of background. Make sure there is enough contrast between the leaf and background fabrics so the points show.

For each block:

1. Cut one 3 1/2" strip and one 2 1/2" strip of each of your chosen background and leaf fabrics for a total of 8 strips. You will have enough left over to piece other blocks.

2. Stack several leaf strips and subcut them at the same time. Do the same with background strips. Subcut pieces from the strips according to the Cutting Chart below. NOTE: *Numbers indicate piecing order for the foundations.*

3. Trace the patterns on page 21

for the small side and large side of the block onto clear template plastic with a Sharpie fine-point marker. Using a copy machine, make one paper copy of each. Mark these copies with a red "O" for original. Turn down the toner on the copy machine to a low setting and make 115 copies of each original pattern. Cut each one out on the outer line. (This number is variable. This quilt has 116 pieced blocks and 16 solid squares. Some of the blocks have solid sections. For these use the small foundation pattern, adding a 1/4" seam allowance, for a template.) *(continued on page 20)*

CUTTING CHART

SMALL SIDE		LARGE SIDE	
Leaf	**Background**	**Leaf**	**Background**
#1 - 3 1/2" x 3"	#2 - 2 1/2" x 1 3/4"	#1 - 2 1/2" x 4"	#2 - 2 1/2" x 4 1/2"
#3 - 2 1/2" x 2"	#4 - 2 1/2" x 2"	#3 - 2 1/2" x 5"	#4 - 2 1/2" x 5 1/2"
#5 - 2 1/2" x 2 1/2"	#6 - 2 1/2" x 3"	#5 - 2 1/2" x 6"	#6 - 3 1/2" x 7"
#7 - 2 1/2" x 3"	#8 - 2 1/2" x 3 1/2"	#7 - 3 1/2" x 8"	#8 - 3 1/2" x 9"
#9 - 2 1/2" x 4 1/2"	#10 - 2 1/2" x 4 1/2"	#9 - 3 1/2" x 9"	#10 - 3 1/2" x 8"
#11 - 3 1/2" x 6"	#12 - 2 1/2" x 6"	#11 - 3 1/2" x 6 1/2"	#12 - 2 1/2" x 6"
#13 - 2 1/2" x 5"	#14 - 2 1/2" x 5"	#13 - 2 1/2" x 5"	#14 - 2 1/2" 4 1/2"
#15 - 2 1/2" x 3"	#16 - 2 1/2" x 4"	#15 - 2 1/2" x 3 1/2"	#16 - 2 1/2" x 3"

Claudia Clark Myers of Duluth, Minnesota, re-drafted the traditional Palm Leaf block to use with her collection of orange, purple, and green batiks in **"Moonshine."** *Claudia says that adding the streak of moonlight made her quilt "come to life."*

(continued from page 18)

4. Piece each foundation in numerical order using the following fabrics in these positions:

odd-numbered sections - leaf fabric

even numbered sections - background NOTE: *Do not trim the excess fabric around the edges yet.*

5. Make an 8" square plastic template (the size of the unfinished block) and using one of the templates, draw the curved seam on the square.

6. Choose a large pieced foundation and a small pieced foundation. Trim the curved edge of each foundation 1/4" beyond the outer line, making a seam allowance.

7. Sew the small side and the large side together along the curved seam. Press the seam toward the small side on the back then press the block on the front.

8. Place the whole-block template on the block, matching the curved line with the curved seam and using a ruler laid along the edge of the template, rotary cut the outer edges of the block. Make 116 blocks.

ASSEMBLY

1. Referring to the photo on page 19, lay out the blocks and 8" assorted print squares in 12 rows of 11. Sew them into rows and join the rows.

2. Sew the 2 1/2" x 40" stripe strips together, end to end, to make a long strip.

3. In the same manner, join the 3 1/4" x 40" dark strips to make a long strip.

4. Cut two 104" lengths and two 96" lengths from each long strip.

5. Sew a 96" stripe strip to a 96" dark strip to make a border. Make 2. Repeat with the 104" strips.

6. Center and sew the 104" strips to the sides of the quilt, placing the stripe strips against the quilt. Start, stop, and backstitch at the 1/4" seamline of the quilt top.

7. Sew the 96" strips to the top and bottom of the quilt in the same manner.

8. Miter the corners in the following way: With the quilt top right side down, lay one border over the other. Using a pencil, draw a straight line at a 45° angle from the inner to the outer corners.

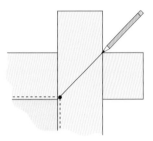

9. Reverse the positions of the borders and mark another corner-to-corner line. With the borders right sides together and the marked seamlines carefully matched, stitch from the inner seamline to the outer corner, backstitching at each end. Open the mitered seam to make sure it lies flat, then trim the excess fabric and press. Repeat for the remaining corners.

10. Remove the paper foundations.

11. Finish the quilt as described in the *General Directions*, using the 2 1/2" x 40" dark print strips for the binding.

Full-size foundations for Moonshine *(The pattern begins on page 18.)*

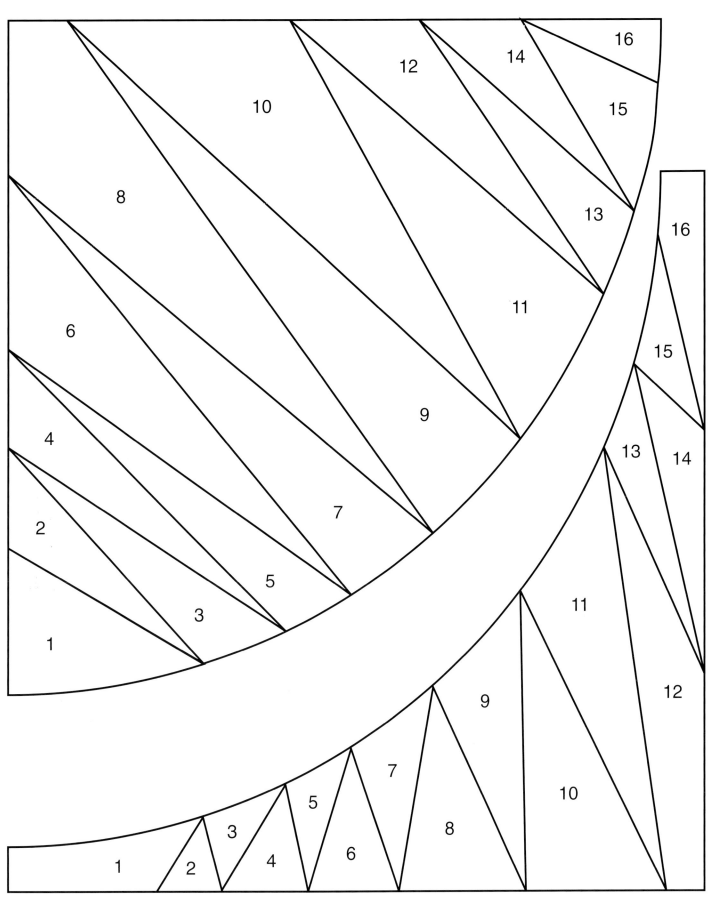

STORM AT SEA

Quilt Size: 87" x 99"

MATERIALS

- Assorted yellow prints from very pale to dark, totaling at least 5 yards
- Assorted blue prints from very pale to navy, totaling at least 7 yards
- 1/2 yard each of 4 yellow prints for the border
- 1 yard navy print for the binding
- 9 yards backing fabric
- 91" x 103" piece of batting

CUTTING

Patterns (on page 25) are full size and include a 1/4" seam allowance as do all dimensions given.

For the large Square-in-a-square blocks:

- Cut 60: 3 3/4" squares, assorted yellow prints, then cut them in half diagonally to yield 120 large triangles
- Cut 62: 4 7/8" squares, assorted blue prints, then cut them in half diagonally to yield 124 large triangles. Set 4 aside for the corner squares.
- Cut 30: 4 1/2" squares, assorted blue prints

For the small Square-in-a-square blocks:

- Cut 84: 2 1/4" squares, assorted yellow prints, then cut them in half diagonally to yield 168 small triangles
- Cut 84: 2 7/8" squares, assorted blue prints, then cut them in half diagonally to yield 168 small triangles
- Cut 42: 2 1/2" squares, assorted blue prints

For the Diamond blocks:

- Cut 194: B, assorted yellow prints
- Cut 194: BR, assorted yellow prints
- Cut 97: A, assorted blue prints

Also:

- Cut 22: 4 1/2" x 8 1/2" rectangles, assorted yellow prints
- Cut 26: 2 1/2" x 8 1/2" strips, assorted yellow prints
- Cut 4: 2 1/2" x 6 1/2" strips, assorted yellow prints
- Cut 2: 4 7/8" squares, yellow prints, then cut them in half diagonally to yield 4 triangles for the corner squares.
NOTE: *If you want each corner to be a different print, cut 4 squares then cut them in half. Use one triangle of each print.* (continued on page 24)

More than one hundred different fabrics give movement to **"Storm at Sea"** by Cheryl Kagen. Though she loves to make miniature quilts, she occasionally makes full-size scrap quilts. Cheryl's border treatment was inspired by Marie Karickoff's quilt "Mer Des Sargasses" which appeared in Storm at Sea—New Quilts from an Old Favorite (AQS,2000.) Ann Shaw of Williamsville, New York, machine quilted Cheryl's quilt with a lovely all-over design.

23

(continued from page 22)

- Cut 22: 2 1/2" x 8 1/2" strips, assorted blue prints
- Cut 4: 2 1/2" x 6 1/2" strips, assorted blue prints
- Cut 4: 2 1/2" x 4 1/2" strips, assorted blue prints
- Cut 44: 4 1/2" squares, assorted blue prints
- Cut 3: 4" x 40" strips, from each of 4 yellow prints, for the border
- Cut 11: 2 1/2" x 40" strips, navy print, for the binding

DIRECTIONS

For the large Square-in-a-square blocks:

1. Sew a yellow print triangle to a 4 1/2" blue print square. Chain piece triangles to the remaining blue squares.

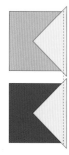

2. Clip the units apart and sew yellow print triangles to the opposite side of each triangle in the same manner.

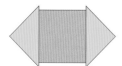

3. Clip them apart and press the seam allowances toward the triangles.

4. Sew yellow print triangles to each of the remaining sides of the blue squares in the same manner.

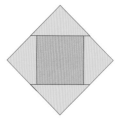

5. Sew 4 blue print triangles to each unit to complete the large blocks.

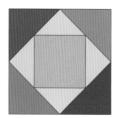

For the small Square-in-a-square blocks:

1. Make 42 blocks in the same manner, using the pieces cut for those blocks.

For the Diamond blocks:

1. Sew a yellow print B to a blue print A, using the dots to align the pieces. Chain sew 97 of these.

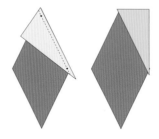

2. Chain sew a yellow print B to the opposite side of each blue print A. Clip the units apart and press the seam allowances toward the B's.

3. Chain sew yellow print BR's to the remaining sides of each unit to complete the Diamond blocks.

For the edge units:

1. Draw a diagonal line from corner to corner on the wrong side of each 4 1/2" blue print square.

2. Place a marked square on one end of a 4 1/2" x 8 1/2" yellow print rectangle, right sides together. Sew on the drawn line. Press the square toward the corner, aligning the edges. Trim the seam allowance to 1/4".

3. Sew a marked square to the opposite end of each rectangle in the same manner. Press and trim, as before, to complete a Flying Geese unit. Make 22.

4. Sew a 2 1/2" x 8 1/2" blue print strip to a 2 1/2" x 8 1/2" yellow print strip. Make 22.

5. Sew a pieced strip to each Flying Geese unit, as shown.

For the corner squares:

1. Sew a large blue print triangle to a yellow print triangle to make a pieced square. Make 4.

2. Sew a 2 1/2" x 4 1/2" blue print strip to the top of each pieced

24

square. Sew a 2 1/2" x 6 1/2" blue print strip to the right side.

3. Sew a 2 1/2" x 6 1/2" yellow print strip to the top of each unit. Sew a 2 1/2" x 8 1/2" yellow print strip to the right side.

ASSEMBLY

1. Referring to the photo on page 23, lay out the large and small Square-in-a-square units, the Diamond units, edge units, and corner squares.

2. Sew the units into rows and join the rows.

3. Sew three 4" x 40" matching yellow print strips together, end to end, to make a border strip. Make 4.

4. Center and sew the border strips to the sides of the quilt. Start and stop 1/4" from the edges of the quilt top and backstitch.

5. Miter the corners in the following way: With the quilt top right side down, lay one border over the other. Using a pencil, draw a straight line at a 45° angle from

the inner to the outer corners.

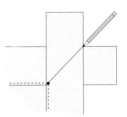

6. Reverse the positions of the borders and mark another corner-to-corner line. With the borders right sides together and the marked seamlines carefully matched, stitch from the inner seamline to the outer corner, backstitching at each end. Open the mitered seam to make sure it lies flat, then trim the excess fabric and press. Repeat for the remaining corners.

7. Finish the quilt as described in the *General Directions*, using the 2 1/2" x 40" navy print strips for the binding.

Full-size patterns for Storm at Sea

(The pattern begins on page 22.)

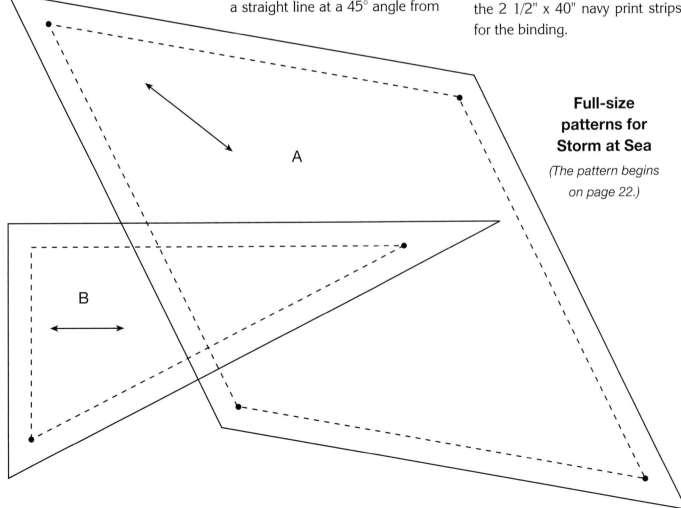

A

B

CIRCLE OF FRIENDSHIP

Quilt Size: 98 1/2" square   **Block Size: 5 1/2" square**

MATERIALS

- Assorted bright prints totaling at least 3 yards
- Black and white prints totaling at least 2 3/4 yards
- 7 1/2 yards black
- 9 yards backing fabric
- 103" square of batting

CUTTING

Dimensions include a 1/4" seam allowance.

- Cut 104: 2" x 6" strips, assorted bright prints
- Cut 28: 2" x 6" strips, assorted black and white print strips

NOTE: *Cut 1 1/2"-wide strips from the remaining bright prints and black and white prints.*

From the 1 1/2"-wide bright print strips:

- Cut 104: 6" strips
- Cut 104: 4 1/2" strips
- Cut 104: 3" strips
- Cut 104: 1 1/2" squares

From the 1 1/2"-wide black and white print strips:

- Cut 28: 6" strips
- Cut 28: 4 1/2" strips
- Cut 28: 3" strips
- Cut 28: 1 1/2" squares
- Cut 144: 2 1/2" squares
- Cut 2 1/2"-wide strips totaling at least 410" when joined for the binding

From the black:

NOTE: *Cut all strips on the lengthwise grain.*

- Cut 2: 6" x 87" strips
- Cut 2: 6" x 76" strips
- Cut 4: 2 1/2" x 72" strips
- Cut 8: 1 3/4" x 54" strips
- Cut 44: 1 1/2" x 47" lengthwise strips; then cut the following lengths from the strips
  132: 6" strips
  132: 4 1/2" strips
  132: 3" strips
  132: 1 1/2" squares
- Cut 4: 6" x 28" strips
- Cut 4: 6" x 22 1/2" strips
- Cut 4: 6" x 17" strips
- Cut 4: 6" x 11 1/2" strips
- Cut 4: 6" squares
- Cut 4: 6" x 30" strips (set aside for the pieced border)

DIRECTIONS

1. Place a 1 1/2" black square on the end of a 1 1/2" x 6" bright strip. Sew from corner to corner, as shown. NOTE: *You might want to draw a line to follow if you find it difficult to sew by "eye".*

2. Press the square toward the corner, aligning the edges. If the edges don't align, adjust the placement of the stitching line. Trim the seam allowance to 1/4". Make 52 and 52 reversed, as shown. Separate them into 2 groups.

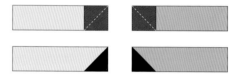

3. Make a pieced strip in the same manner, using a 1 1/2" bright square and a 1 1/2" x 6" black strip, as shown. Make 52 and 52 reversed, as shown.

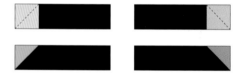

4. Place a 1 1/2" x 3" black strip on a 1 1/2" x 4 1/2" bright strip, right sides together and aligning the corners. Sew from corner to corner, as shown. Make 52 and 52 reversed.

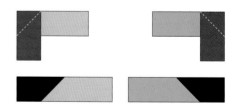

5. Make a pieced strip in the same manner, using a 1 1/2" x 3" bright strip and a 1 1/2" x 4 1/2" black strip, as shown. Make 52 and 52 reversed. *(continued on page 31)*

While on a business trip in Jerome, Arizona, Shelley Knapp and her husband, Randy, went fabric shopping with fellow quiltmaker Leigh Hay-Martin. The three challenged each other to buy 10 fat quarters to combine into one quilt. Randy chose the black and white prints, while Shelley and Leigh chose the same bright fabrics. They all decided that black was necessary to bring it all together in **"Circle of Friendship,"** *also know as "The Jerome Quilt."*

COMPLEMENTARY COLORS

Quilt Size: 41 1/4" x 56 1/4"   **Block Size: 15" square**

MATERIALS

- 3/4 yard each of solid red, orange, and yellow (warm colors) and green, blue, and purple (cool colors)
- 1/8 yard each of 8 prints in each color (red, orange, yellow, green, blue, and purple)
- 3/4 yard binding fabric
- 2 5/8 yards backing fabric
- 45" x 60" piece of batting
- Fusible web

CUTTING

Patterns (on page 30) are full size and include a 1/4" seam allowance as do all dimensions given.

From each 1/8-yard print:
- Cut 4: center pieces
- Cut 1: end piece and one reversed end piece
- Cut 1: 2 3/8" x 15 1/2" strip
- Cut 1: 2 3/8" x 17 3/8" strip (orange, yellow, blue, and purple only)

From each solid:
- Cut 1: 16" background square
- Cut 8: 4 1/4" squares
- Cut 8: 2" squares
- Cut 8: 2 1/2" circles NOTE: *Fuse web to the wrong side*

of these fabrics before cutting circles. Substitute 2" squares for some circles, if desired. Refer to the quilt for inspiration.
Also:
- Cut 6: 3" x 40" strips, for the binding

DIRECTIONS

1. Work with one color at a time to make each ring. Stitch 4 center pieces together to make an arc. Stitch an end piece and a reversed end piece to each arc. Make 8 arcs of each color.

2. Carefully press the seam allowances open. Stabilize the edges by stay stitching 3/16" from the curved edges.

3. Choose 8 arcs of one color family. Stitch an analogous 2" corner square to each end of 2 arcs. Stitch corner squares to the ends of 2 of the remaining arcs.
NOTE: *Analogous colors are next to one another on the color wheel.* Stitch purple squares to 2 blue arcs and green squares

to 2 blue arcs. Stitch orange and purple squares to red arcs, green and orange squares to yellow arcs, red and blue squares to purple arcs, red and yellow squares to orange arcs, and yellow and blue squares to green arcs. Refer to the photo as necessary.

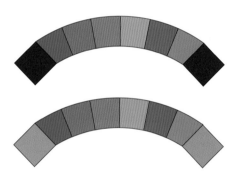

4. Stitch an arc without corner squares to one with squares to make a melon shape. Stitch only to the seamline on the inner edge and backstitch.

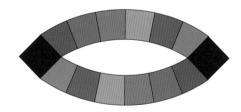

5. Join 4 melon shapes at the corner squares to make a Double

(continued on page 30)

*After sleeping under her Grandmother's Double Wedding Ring quilt for several years, Mary Russell created her own contemporary version in bold **"Complementary Colors"**. To learn more about Mary or to purchase her Double Wedding Ring rulers, visit her website at www.mary-russell.com.*

(continued from page 28)

Wedding Ring, again stitching only to the seamline on the inner edge and backstitching. Make 6.

6. Appliqué each Wedding Ring to a complementary 16" background square, turning under a 1/4" seam allowance. Combine red and green, purple and yellow, and blue and orange.

7. Press the blocks on the wrong side and trim each one to 15 1/2" square, keeping the appliqué centered.

For the Border Squares:

1. Fuse a circle or 2" square to each of the 4 1/4" squares. Place the warm-color shapes on the cool-color squares and the cool-color shapes on the warm-color squares. Machine appliqué the edges of the shapes.

ASSEMBLY

1. Lay out the blocks in 3 rows of 2. Sew them into rows and join the rows.

2. Place the 2 3/8"-wide strips around the quilt center, as shown below.

3. Sew the strips together into 4 borders.

4. Sew the right-side border to the quilt, aligning the top edges. Stop stitching about 1" before the bottom edge of the quilt.

5. Sew the top border to the quilt, then the left-side border, then the bottom border.

6. Complete the seam for the right-side border.

7. Lay out 13 border squares, beginning and ending with cool-color squares and alternating cool and warm. Make 2. Press the seam allowances open.

8. Lay out 11 squares, beginning and ending with warm-color squares. Make 2. Press.

9. Stitch the long borders to the sides of the quilt. Stitch the short borders to the top and bottom.

10. Finish the quilt as described in the *General Directions*, using the 3" x 40" strips for the binding.

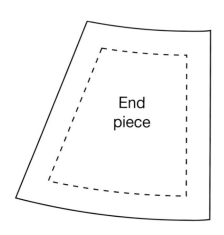

End piece

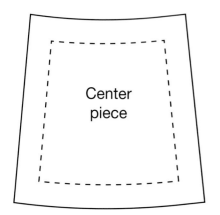

Center piece

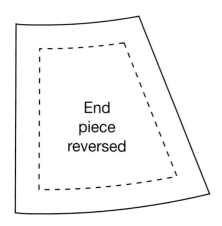

End piece reversed

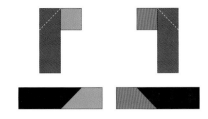

6. Lay out one of each type of strip from one group and one 2" x 6" bright print strip. Join the strips to make a block. Make 52 and 52 reversed.

7. Make 14 of each type of block using the black and white strips and squares and the remaining black strips and squares.

ASSEMBLY

1. Referring to the Assembly Diagram, lay out 56 bright blocks (28 of each type), the black and white blocks, the 6"-wide black strips (except the 30"-long strips), and the 6" black squares.
2. Sew the strips and squares into rows and join the rows.
3. Measure the quilt through the center. Trim 2 of the 2 1/2" x 72" black strips to that measurement. Sew them to opposite sides of the

quilt.
4. Measure the quilt, including the borders. Trim the remaining 2 1/2" x 72" black strips to that measurement and sew them to the quilt.
5. Sew thirty-five 2 1/2" black and white squares together to make a border. Make 2. Sew them to opposite sides of the quilt, adjusting to fit if necessary.
6. Sew thirty-seven 2 1/2" black and white squares together to make a border. Make 2. Sew them to the quilt.
7. Measure the quilt. Trim the 6" x 76" black strips to that measurement. Sew them to opposite sides of the quilt.
8. Trim the 6" x 87" black strips to fit the quilt and sew them to the remaining sides.
9. Sew 2 bright blocks together to make a border unit, as shown. Make 24.

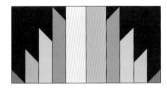

10. Sew 6 border units together. Make 4.
11. Cut each 6" x 30" black strip into one 18" section and one 12" section.
12. Sew a 6" x 12" black strip to each end of a border section. Make 2.
13. Measure the width of the

quilt. Trim the borders to that measurement. Be sure to keep the blocks centered by trimming an equal amount from each end of the border. Sew them to opposite sides of the quilt.
14. Sew the 6" x 18" strips to the ends of the remaining borders. Trim them as before and sew them to the remaining sides of the quilt.
15. Sew two 1 3/4" x 54" black strips together, end to end, to make a border strip. Make 4.
16. Measure the quilt and trim two borders to that measurement. Sew them to opposite sides of the quilt.
17. Trim the remaining borders to fit and sew them to the quilt.
18. Finish the quilt as described in the *General Directions*, using the 2 1/2"-wide black and white strips for the binding.

1/4 of the Assembly Diagram

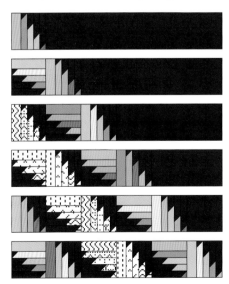

About the Patterns

Read through the pattern directions before cutting fabric. Yardage requirements are based on fabric with a useable width of 42". Pattern directions are given in step-by-step order. If you are sending your quilt to a professional machine quilter, consult the quilter regarding the necessary batting and backing size for your quilt.

Fabrics

We suggest using 100% cotton. Wash fabric in warm water with mild detergent. Do not use fabric softener. Dry fabric on a warm-to-hot setting. Press with a hot dry iron to remove any wrinkles.

Templates

Template patterns are full size and unless otherwise noted, include a 1/4" seam allowance. The solid line is the cutting line; the dashed line is the stitching line. Templates for hand piecing do not include a seam allowance.

Piecing

For machine piecing, sew 12 stitches per inch, exactly 1/4" from the edge of the fabric. To make accurate piecing easier, mark the throat plate with a piece of tape 1/4" to the right of the point where the needle pierces the fabric.

Foundation Piecing

Foundation piecing is a method for making blocks with a high degree of accuracy. Foundation patterns are full size and do not include a seam allowance. For each foundation, trace all of the lines and numbers onto paper. You will need one foundation for each block or part of a block as described in the pattern. The solid lines are stitching lines. The fabric pieces you select do not have to be cut precisely. Be generous when cutting fabric pieces as excess fabric will be trimmed away after sewing. Your goal is to cut a piece that covers the numbered area and extends into surrounding areas after seams are stitched. Generally, fabric pieces should be large enough to extend 1/2" beyond the seamline on all sides before stitching. For very small sections, or sections without angles, 1/4" may be sufficient.

Place fabric pieces on the unmarked side of the foundation and stitch on the marked side. Center the first piece, right side up, over position 1 on the unmarked side of the foundation. Hold the foundation up to a light to make sure that the raw edges of the fabric

extend at least 1/2" beyond the seamline on all sides. Hold this first piece in place with a small dab of glue or a pin, as desired. Place the fabric for position 2 on the first piece, right sides together. Turn the foundation over, and sew on the line between 1 and 2, extending the stitching past the beginning and end of the line by a few stitiches on both ends. Trim the seam allowance to 1/4". Fold the position 2 piece back, right side up, and press. Continue adding pieces to the foundation in the same manner until all positions are covered and the block is complete. Trim the fabric 1/4" beyond the edge of the foundation.

To avoid disturbing the stitches, do not remove the paper until the blocks have been joined together and all the borders have been added, unless instructed to remove them sooner in the pattern. The paper will be perforated from the stitching and can be gently pulled free. Use tweezers to carefully remove small sections of the paper, if necessary.

Pressing

Press with a dry iron. Press seam allowances toward the darker of the two pieces whenever possible. Otherwise, trim away 1/16" from the darker seam allowance to prevent it from shadowing through. Press abutting seams in opposite directions. Press all blocks, sashings, and borders before assembling the quilt top.

FINISHING YOUR QUILT
Binding

Cut the binding strips with the grain for straight-edge quilts. Binding for quilts with curved edges must be cut on the bias. To make 1/2" finished binding, cut 2 1/2"-wide strips. Sew strips together with diagonal seams; trim and press seam allowance open.

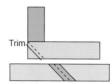

Fold the strip in half lengthwise, wrong side in, and press. Position the strip on the right side of the quilt top, aligning the raw edges of the binding with the edge of the quilt top. Leaving 6" of the binding strip free and beginning a few inches from one corner, stitch the binding to the quilt with a 1/4" seam allowance measuring from the raw edge of the quilt top. When you reach a corner, stop stitching 1/4" from the edge of the quilt top

and backstitch. Clip the threads and remove the quilt from the machine. Fold the binding up and away from the quilt, forming a 45° angle, as shown.

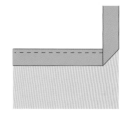

Keeping the angled fold secure, fold the binding back down. This fold should be even with the edge of the quilt top. Begin stitching at the fold.

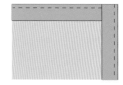

Continue stitching around the quilt in this manner to within 6" of the starting point. To finish, fold both strips back along the edge of the quilt so that the folded edges meet about 3" from both lines of the stitching and the binding lies flat on the quilt. Finger press to crease the folds. Measure the width of the folded binding. Cut the strips that distance beyond the folds. (In this case 1 1/4" beyond the folds.)

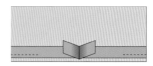

Open both strips and place the ends at right angles to each other, right sides together. Fold the bulk of the quilt out of your way. Join the strips with a diagonal seam as shown.

Trim the seam allowance to 1/4" and press it open. Refold the strip wrong side in. Place the binding flat against the quilt, and finish stitching it to the quilt. Trim excess batting and backing so that the binding edge will be filled with batting when you fold the binding to the back of the quilt. Blindstitch the binding to the back, covering the seamline.

Remove visible markings. Make a label that includes your name, the date the quilt was completed, and any other pertinent information, and stitch it to the back of your quilt.